60 DAYS TO YOUR BEST RUGBY

A COMPLETE Strength Training and Nutrition Guide to Get Stronger, Faster and Fitter

Mariana Correa

Copyright Page

2016 60 Days to Your Best Rugby
ISBN 9781533670335

Acknowledgement

To my team, thank you for always pushing me to excel and challenge my goals.

About the author

Mariana Correa is a certified professional coach and former professional tennis player. Mariana reached a career high of 26 in the world in juniors with wins over Anna Ivanovich (former #1 WTA in the world) and many other top 100 WTA players.

She competed successfully all over the world in over 26 countries and hundreds of cities including in London for Wimbledon, Paris for the French Open and in Australia for the world championships. She also represented Ecuador in Fed Cup, where the team reached the finals in their group.

During her career she was awarded the fair play award many times, proving to be not only an excellent player, but also a role model for other athletes.

Mariana is also a certified sports nutritionist with years of experience in proper nutrition and hydration for high performance athletes. She combines her love and knowledge in sports in this book to provide you with all the information you need to succeed.

Description

60 Days to your Best Rugby is the best book to improve your speed, strength, confidence and nutrition in only two months.
With a detailed day by day training session you will play and look better. Anyone can be their best it will take hard work and dedication, and the right training program. This strength training guide is complete with hard core warm ups, body specific workouts, plyometric exercises, ab training, cool downs, and tips for your best Rugby yet. Keeping your body strong and injury free.
Nutrition is a big part of any training program, remember when you think you're done training, you're not done training, at least not until you've put some nutrients back into your body. You will find included a full chapter with 50 Paleo recipes for any time of day, allowing your body to fully replenish you for your following workout.
After completing these 60 days you will be able to: move faster, lose unwanted body fat, fight stronger, increase muscle growth, strike

with power, increase your endurance, improve your health and nutrition and much more.

Table of Contents

Introduction

Secrets to SUCCESS

"Whatever you can do, or dream you can, begin it. Boldness has genius, power and magic in it. "J. Goethe
If you dream of greatness prepare adequately. Ask any top professional how hard they have worked to get to where they are, the answer never seizes to amaze. Countless hours have been spent in the gym before any athlete lifts a trophy, proud of their achievement.
After preparing and training to reach a specific goal, the satisfaction you feel when you achieve your goal is fulfilling and motivates you to strive for more. It truly is one of the best feelings in the world.
Nowadays everything is becoming even more demanding. Athletes need to be stronger, fitter and faster. There is no substitute for hours of practicing. Great form, mental toughness and mighty strength weren't granted to any top athlete. They all worked hard to earn every bit of what they have. This is something you

definitely have to understand if you have the desire to become a champion.

Nothing will ever come for free or granted. Do you love it enough to fight day in and out to reach your goals?

Yes! Wonderful, then let's get started.

Chapter 1:
Goal Setting

"Set daily, monthly and long term goals and dreams. Don't ever be afraid to dream too big. Nothing is impossible. If you believe in yourself, you can achieve it. "Natasha Liukin - Olympic champion

Goal setting is the first step along the route to your Rugby ideals.

Success in any field does not happen by chance. It is the result of deliberate decisions, conscious efforts, and immense persistence.

You must first know where you want to go and how you are going to get there. This is important not only in Rugby, but also in life.

By helping yourself establish goals in Rugby, you will later use these guidelines when setting goals in your personal life as well.

In order to set on the correct path you must first know where you would like to go. Set your goals high, and strive for excellence.

A journey of meaning in Rugby, or any other sport for that matter, requires goals and specific plans to achieve them. Countless of the most successful individuals in the world lay their success down to knowing what they wanted and where they were going.

Well-structured goals and strategies are the single most important base in the long-term effectiveness and sustainability of your career. Goals need to be constantly reappraised, and refocused. Time goes by, new ideals surface, always reaching for the moon to land on a star. You must embrace challenges. Make these goals fun and engaging. This will motivate you and impulse you in the correct direction.

Be **SMART** with your goal setting.

Specific- the more specific your goals are, the easier it will be to reach them.

Measureable - if you can quantify the progress, the results will be clearer. Establish your goals so you may see your progress in numbers.

Attainable - make the goals realistic. We are boosting your confidence by every goal that you reach. We need to make these goals accessible to you; they must be challenging, but still be attainable.

Relevant - the goal must help you move in the direction of larger ideals. It must make sense.

Time bound - goals have a better chance to be achieved when there is time frame in which they must be achieved.

When establishing goals we must also consider the following suggestions.

1. Few goals. Do not overwhelm yourself with goals; select a few goals at a time. Your energy and focus is designed to concentrate on a select couple to excel.

2. Flexibility. Goals are not set in stone. They may change, adapt and evolve. Physical abilities, personal circumstances, and time constraints, may sometimes require adjusting our goals. This is not giving up on the goal, but merely adapting to any new situations which are impeding you to achieve it.

3. Difficulties. There will always be road blocks along the way. But these will only make you value your achieved goals even more. When a task is challenging, more value is automatically placed on the outcome. When something is handed to you it doesn't have the same value as when you earned it.

Keep a training log

Dreams are only dreams until you write them down.
Then they become goals.

Keep a journal with you so you may write down your goals and training logs.

Recording your activity is a great way to motivate yourself as well by being able to look back at all the goals that have already achieved.

It is very hard for anybody to memorize every milestone, achievement or setbacks in their journey towards becoming a star this is why these must be recorded in a journal.

Another benefit of keeping a training journal would be the motivation and confidence the journal provides. It provides you with focus and belief that you have worked hard to achieve your goals.

In the daily entries it would be good idea to include:

- Time and place of training

- Details of training

- Comments on how training went

- Purpose of training

- Feelings before/after training

- Goals achieved

In the competition entries it would be good idea to include:

- Time and location competition took

  place

- Goals achieved before competition

- Feelings before and after competing

- Comments on how competition went

- Were the goals set achieved

- Improvements for the next competition

These journals should be written in a calm and trusting environment. Remember to be honest and real, but at the same time maintain a positive view to the future and log in improvements and rewards.

Chapter 2:
Train to be Perfect

"Success is no accident. It is hard work, perseverance, learning, studying, sacrifice, and most of all, love of what you are doing or learning to do." Pele

No matter what you are striving to be good at in life, it will require dedication and hard work. Anything you want to achieve can be achieved; it all comes down to how bad you want it, and how hard you are willing to work to get there.

Look at those professional athletes you admire so much, stop and ask yourself, how did they get there? What makes them different from everyone else? What did they do that made them so good?

They all have one thing in common, they have practiced hundreds of thousands of hours at a high level of intensity. That is their big secret, they worked a lot harder than anyone else.

If you want to be excellent in anything in life, it's going to involve persistently pushing past your comfort zone, as well as frustration, struggle, obstacles and disappointments. This is true as long as you want to continue to advance and sustain a high level of excellence.

The reward is being the best in life at something you've earned through your own hard work and that can be incredibly satisfying.

You will gain so much from hard work. Your self-esteem will soar and physical capabilities will increase dramatically. Remember in life and in sports nothing is ever handed to you, everything must be earned.

Quality over quantity

An important concept to consider in training is not always volume, but the quality in that volume. Instead of wasting time and energy be efficient with your time. Make sure you are working toward your set goals and objectives. Each workout should be a step forward, a superior practice.

In order to achieve a superior practice you must have a smart practice. A smart practice would be a training session in which every exercise is done with the purpose to improve.

Training efficiently and effectively, not with the purpose pass time and wear yourself down.

A single hour of practice at the highest intensity will be of more value than 3 hours at a half effort. Any athlete will benefit more from a short, concentrated practice with purpose, than on long practices simply wasting time, money and energy.

A good program will have each training session in a step by step basis, as you progress you will move to the next level. A coach will identify what you need and as soon as this is met, you will continue to advance to the next phase.

Not everyone has the same needs. A correct program will identify your level and place you in the adequate setting.

Let's take as an example a cake that is taken out of the oven too soon. It won't be ready. If you are rushed you will not develop adequately either. You must go through phases in which you will mature and grow in order to move forward.

How much should I be training?

There is no precise amount of hours and days you should be training. Everyone has a different endurance and body type. But, a good estimate for the amount of hours you should be training and what the purpose of your training would be 1 ½ to 3 hours per day.

Keep in mind. Overtraining will only end up with a burned out, fatigued and physically underdeveloped you.

Chapter 3:
Prepare your Body for Battle

Warm up and Cool down

Warm up and cool down should occur at the **beginning and end of each practice** and match. Both are **essential** for any athlete in order to perform better.

Warm up consists of the following:

1) A lite jog around the field or in place for 3-5 minutes, the distance and duration depend on the athletes level.

2) Dynamic flexibility exercises. Consisting on flexibility in motion, for example lunging from one side to another 8-10 times.
   The best way to gauge if the athlete is warmed up would be a bit of perspiration and a rise in heart rate.

   The benefits of warming up well are many such as:

- Increased Blood Temperature. This increase of temperature also increases the volume of oxygen that is made available to muscles in activity, enhancing performance.

- Increased Body Temperature. This improves muscle flexibility, reducing the risk of injuries from strains and pulls.

- Mental Preparation. A good warm up helps clear the mind, and increase focus.

Keep in mind that a warm up is just a warm up and not a "practice session." The key of a good warm up is to loosen up your muscles, increase temperature and focus the mind. It's not the time to begin working on mechanics or issues that should be addressed in practice. Following a good event or match, cool down is the following step.

Cool down is exactly as it sounds we are decreasing heart rate, slowly lowering body temperature and reducing the risk of muscle soreness.

The cool down should consist of a jog that decreases in speed down to a lite walk for approximately 3-5 minutes.

Followed by static stretching. Static stretching would be stretching exercises in which you are holding the position for 15-30 seconds to relax the muscles. This stretching addresses each muscle 2-3 times for 15-30 seconds each time relaxing and breathing throughout. This is how the best in the world prepare, allow this mindset to become a habit for you. Later in your career your body will thank you.

Flexibility

Flexibility refers to the body's capacity to successfully bend and move without injury. Improving flexibility allows the body to increase the range of motion at a specific location as well as improving stability. Just like other physical motor skills, flexibility is a constant process rather than a static point of achievement, and the best way to keep the body flexible is to continue to work on it. Flexibility training is an important part of your overall fitness level, these are some of the many benefits through flexibility.

- Prevents injuries. Studies show that up to 65% of injuries can be prevented with stretching before and after exercising.
- Quicker recovery after exercise.
- Decrease in tension.
- Better balance and coordination.
- Improved posture.
- Promotes healthy lifestyle practices.

We are born flexible. As we grow older we begin to lose their flexibility. Inactivity for long periods can also reduce flexibility and lead to tightness over time.

Do's:

- Remember to breathe slowly and evenly. This will help deliver the proper oxygen to your muscles.
- Stretch uniformly focusing on each move and use proper form.
- Hold the stretch for approximately 30 seconds will breathing deeply
- Maintain good posture. Learn how to perform each stretch properly before you begin.

Don'ts:

- Do not bounce. Use slow movements. Too much stress is placed on tendons and muscles if you are bouncing to push yourself outside your normal range of motion.
- Do not overstretch and push your body to the point of pain.

- Don't overextend your joints. Hyperextending further than you can, will actually lead to injuries.

What would normally be considered an off day of training or matches, or in other words a day in which you have no training scheduled it's recommended to stretch. Off days are days to work on flexibility and relaxation. Even it's only 30 minutes, stretching is extremely important and will help you very much. I encourage you to stretch on your down time it will take away your stress, and relax your body.

Now that we have prepared your body, let's prepare your mind. The best way to work on your mind would be through imagination. Imagining and visualizing all that could and will one day be.

Visualization

"We are only limited by our imagination and our belief that what we have imagined is possible." - Seth M. Quealy

In order to achieve something you must first see it in your mind. Imagine yourself executing a task to perfection. Everything you can dream of, you can achieve. Countless events are won or lost before even appearing there. The confidence and the vision you have of winning will help you achieve victories. Visualization develops the mental aspect of the game, which plays a big role in performance. Sports Psychologists are using visualization to train athletes to strengthen their mental abilities. Visualization or imagery would be your ability to create events or happenings in your mind. This is something we actually do in our day to day lives without even realizing.

Some purposes of visualization are:
- Improving technique
- Improving Tactics and strategies
- Improving Mental preparation.

Let's setup an example of how a visualization exercise would work.

1. Make sure you are in a quiet and comfortable place. Relax your breathing and close your eyes.

2. Engage your senses. Look at the colors around you, the public, or your coach. Hear the sounds you would normally hear, such as breathing or cheering.

3. Feel yourself improving, your best technique, strength and intensity.

4. Add emotions to the exercise. Notice how happy you are. Feel the rush and adrenaline from performing. The confident image that you portray is glowing.

5. See yourself achieving your goals. Whatever it is you're striving for, do it now. Feel the satisfaction of your effort. You earned it.

6. Try to log in everything around you and everything inside you. Notice the public, how you felt, and your body language.

When the time comes in real life it will be easier for your mind and body to recreate these positive actions because you have already achieved your goals, even if it was only in your mind.

Chapter 4:
60 DAYS TO BE YOUR BEST

DAY 1   (reps/sets)

Jump rope (double unders) 20 min

Bench press	5/4
Military press	5/3
Dumbbell front raise	10 (each arm)/3
Dumbbell lateral raise	10/3
Bent over lateral raise	10/3
Triceps pushdown	10/5

Dips till failure

Choose a weight on bench press and military press which allows you to perform 5 reps with a good form. Rest about 30 seconds between sets, and 1 minute between exercises, expect on bench press and military press, where you should rest 45 seconds between sets, and 1 minute and 15 seconds between exercises. Go straight for the dips right after you have finished your last set of triceps pushdowns.

Day 2

Sit ups   10/5

Knee ups 10/4

Heel touches 20/2 (Alternate sides)

L-sit till failure

Rest 15 seconds between sets and 25 seconds between exercises on your ab workout.

Day 3

Deadlift   5/4

Pull ups 10/5

Dumbbell row 10 (each side)/3

Barbell curls 10/5

Reverse barbell curls 10/3

Handstand Wall Walks 3/3

Choose a weight in deadlifts which allows you to perform a 5 reps with a good form. Go heavy on dumbbell rows. Rest 20 seconds between sets and 45 seconds between exercises, except on deadlifts and db rows, where you should rest 30 seconds between sets and 1 minute between exercises.

Day 4

Sit ups   15/4

Knee ups 15/3

Heel touches 20/2 (Alternate sides)

"Rocky" Sprinting Stairs 20 min

Single Leg Plyo squat Jump 10/2

Rest 15 seconds between sets and 25 seconds between exercises on your ab workout, and 25 seconds between sets.

Day 5

Jump rope (double unders) 20 min

Back Squat 5/3

Leg press   10/4

Leg extension 10/3

Romanian deadlift 10/3

Seated calf raise 20/3
Sled Push Sprint AMRAP

Choose a weight on back squat which allows you to perform 5 reps with a good form. Rest 35 seconds between sets and 50 seconds between exercises, except on back squats, where you should rest 45 seconds between sets, and 1 minute and 15 seconds between exercises.

Day 6

Bench press 5/4   +2.5kg, or 10/2

Military press   5/3   +2.5kg or 8/2

Dumbbell front raise   15 (each arm)/3

Dumbbell lateral raise   15/3

Bent over lateral raise   15/3

Dips till failure

Add 2.5 kg to your bench press and military press. If you can't perform 5 reps with the increased weight, double the amount of reps on one set, and increase the weight on your next workout. Rest 30 seconds between sets, and 1 minute between exercises, expect on bench press and military press, where you should rest 1 minute between sets, and 1 minute and 30 seconds between exercises. Try to perform more dips that you did on your last workout.

Day 7

Sit ups   15/5

Knee ups 15/4

Heel touches 20/3 (Alternate sides)
Medicine Ball Crunches AMRAP

Running:

2200m with moderate speed

Sprint 60m as fast as you can

15m as fast as you can/5

Rest 15 seconds between sets and 25 seconds between
exercises on your ab workout. Do not rest after 2200m, go straight for the sprint. Rest 2 minutes after sprinting, and go for the next exercise. Rest about 10 seconds between sets on 15m.

Day 8

Yoga/ Flexibility Day

Use this day to recover from your workouts. You will warm up lightly with a 5 minute jog and proceed to stretch every muscle in your body. Hold each stretch for 30 seconds and repeat each stretch 3 times. Try to increase your flexibility with each stretch.

Or

1 hour of any kind of yoga training you would like. This will help you increase your flexibility and muscle recovery.

Day 9

Jump rope (double unders) 10 min

Sit ups   20/4

Knee ups 20/4

Russian twist 30/3 (Alternate sides)

L-sit till failure

Rest 15 seconds between sets and 25 seconds between exercises on your ab workout. Rest 25 seconds between sets. Try to maintain your L-sit longer than you did on your last workout.

Day 10

35 minutes of running with a moderate speed

Single Leg Plyo squat Jump 12/2

Back Squat 5/3 +2.5kg or 8/2

Leg press   12/4

Leg extension 15/2

Romanian deadlift 15/3

Seated calf raise 30/3

Add 2.5 kg to your back squat. If you can't perform 5 reps with increased weight, double the amount of reps on one set and increase the weight on your next workout. Rest 35 seconds between sets and 50 seconds between exercises, except on back squats, where you should rest 45 seconds between sets, and 1 minute and 15 seconds between exercises.

Day 11

Plyometric Pushups 25/4

Bench press   5/4   +2.5kg, or 10/2

Military press   5/3   +2.5kg or 8/2

Dumbbell front raise   15 (each arm)/4

Dumbbell lateral raise   15/4

Bent over lateral raise   15/4

Triceps pushdown   15/4

Dips till failure

Add 2.5 kg to your bench press and military press. If you can't perform 5 reps with the increased weight, double the amount of reps on one set, and increase the weight on your next workout. Rest 30 seconds between sets, and 1 minute between exercises, expect on bench press and military press, where you should rest 1 minute between sets, and 1 minute and 30 seconds between exercises. Try to perform more dips that you did on your last workout.

Day 12

Jack knives   10/5

Hanging knee raises 10/5

Side plank   for 30 seconds (each side)

Medicine Ball Crunches AMRAP

Rest 15 seconds between sets and 25 seconds between ab exercises. Remember to keep your torso steady as possible on hanging knee raises.

Day 13

Deadlift   5/4 +2.5 kg or 10/2

Pull ups 12/5

Barbell bent over row 12 /4

Cable curls 12/5 + drop set 20 reps

Reverse barbell curls 12/4

Add 2.5 kg to your deadlift. If you can't perform 5 reps with increased weight, double the amount of reps on one set, and increase the weight on your next workout. Dropset means that once you reach muscle failure with heavier weight, you reduce the weight and perform more repetitions until you reach muscle failure again. Go straight for the drop set until you have finished your last set of cable curls. Rest 45 seconds between sets and 1 minute between exercises, except on deadlifts and bent over rows, where you should rest 45 seconds between sets and 1 minute and 30 seconds between exercises.

Day 14

Jump rope (double unders) 20 min

Jack knives   15/4

Hanging knee raises 15/4

Side plank   40 seconds (each side)

Rest 10 seconds between sets and 30 seconds between exercises on your ab workout. Rest 20 seconds between sets.

Day 15

30 minutes of running with a moderate speed

Sled Push Sprint AMRAP

Back Squat 5/3 +2.5kg or 8/2

Leg press   10/4 +5kg or 20/4

Dumbbell lunges 15/3 (Alternate legs)

Romanian deadlift 10/4 +5kg or 20/3

Seated calf raise 10/4 +5kg or 40/2

Add 2.5 kg to your back squat, and 5kg to your seated calf raise, Romanian deadlift, and leg press. If you can't perform most of the reps properly with increased weight, double the amount of reps on one set and increase the weight on your next workout. Go heavy on DB lunges. Rest 45 seconds between sets and 1 minute between exercises, except on back squats, where you should rest 1 minute between sets, and 1 minute and 30 seconds between exercises.

Day 16

Yoga/ Flexibility Day

Use this day to recover from your workouts. You will warm up lightly with a 5 minute jog and proceed to stretch every muscle in your body. Hold each stretch for 30 seconds and repeat each stretch 3 times. Try to increase your flexibility with each stretch.

Or

1 hour of any kind of yoga training you would like. This will help you increase your flexibility and muscle recovery.

Day 17

Jack knives   20/3

Hanging knee raises 20/3

Side plank   50 seconds (each side)

Running:

2400m with moderate speed

Sprint 60m as fast as you can

15m as fast as you can/6

Rest 10 seconds between sets and 30 seconds between ab exercises. Keep your torso as steady as possible on Hanging knee raises. Do not rest after 2400 m on running, go straight for the sprint. Rest 2 minutes before going for the 15m, and rest 10 seconds between sets.

Day 18

Deadlift   5/8 +2.5 kg or 10/2

Chin ups with bicep focus 10/8

Reverse barbell curls 10/4 +2.5kg

Handstand Wall Walks 6/3

Plyometric Pushups 20/5

Add 2.5 kg to your deadlift. If you can't perform 5 reps with increased weight, double the amount of reps on one set, and increase the weight on your next workout. Focus on really squeezing your biceps on chin ups Rest 30 seconds between sets and 1 minute and 30 seconds between exercises, except on deadlifts where you should rest 1 minute between sets and 2 minutes between exercises.

Day 19

"Rocky" Sprinting Stairs 30 min.

Jack knives   20/4

Hanging knee raises 20/4

Side plank   1 minute (each side)

Front Plank 2 min/2

Rest 10 seconds between sets and 30 seconds between exercises on your ab workout. Rest 25 seconds between sets.

Day 20

35 minutes of running with a moderate speed

Back Squat 5/7 +2.5kg or 8/4

Dumbbell lunges 20/3 (Alternate legs)

Romanian deadlift 10/5

Seated calf raise 15/4

Single Leg Plyo squat Jump 10/3

Add 2.5 kg to your back squat. If you can't perform most of the reps properly with increased weight, double the amount of reps on one set and increase the weight on your next workout. Go heavy on DB lunges. Rest 30 seconds between sets and 1 minute between exercises, except on back squats, where you should rest 1 minute between sets, and 1 minute and 30 seconds between exercises.

Day 21

Weighted dips with chest focus 12/4

Bench press   5/4   +2.5kg, or 10/2

Military press   5/3   +2.5kg or 8/2

Dumbbell front raise   12/3

Dumbbell lateral raise 12/3

Bent over lateral raise 12/3

Bodyweight triceps extensions 10/3

Lean slightly forward on dips to get a better chest activation. Add 2.5 kg to your bench press and military press. If you can't perform 5 reps with the increased weight, double the amount of reps on one set, and increase the weight on your next workout. Rest 30 seconds between sets, and 1 minute between exercises, expect on bench press and military press, where you should rest 1 minute between sets, and 2 minutes between exercises.

Day 22

Jump rope (double unders) 30 min

Medicine Ball Crunches AMRAP

Jack knives   30/3

Hanging leg raises 10/3

Side plank 1 minute and 15 seconds (each side)

Rest 15 seconds between sets and 30 seconds between ab exercises.

Day 23

Deadlift   5/4 +2.5 kg or 10/2

Straight arm pulldowns 15/4

Chin ups with bicep focus 15/6

Reverse barbell curls 10/4

Add 2.5 kg to your deadlift. If you can't perform 5 reps with increased weight, double the amount of reps on one set, and increase the weight on your next workout. Focus on really squeezing your biceps on chin ups Rest 45 seconds between sets and 1 minute and 15 seconds between exercises, except on deadlifts where you should rest 1 minute between sets and 2 minutes between exercises.

Day 24

"Rocky" Sprinting Stairs 20 min.

Jack knives   30/3

Hanging leg raises 10/4

Side plank 1 minute and 30 seconds (each side)

Single Leg Burpee (5 each leg) 10/3

Rest 15 seconds between sets and 30 seconds between exercises on your ab workout. Rest 30 seconds between sets.

Day 25

Yoga/ Flexibility Day

Use this day to recover from your workouts. You will warm up lightly with a 5 minute jog and proceed to stretch every muscle in your body. Hold each stretch for 30 seconds and repeat each stretch 3 times. Try to increase your flexibility with each stretch.

Or

1 hour of any kind of yoga training you would like. This will help you increase your flexibility and muscle recovery.

Day 26

Jump rope (double unders) 20 min

Weighted dips with chest focus 15/4

Bench press   8/4

Military press   10/10

Lateral pushups   20/1 (alternate
                    sides)

Plyometric Pushups 15/6

Lean slightly forward on dips to get a better chest activation. Try to keep the same weight on bench press and military press as you did on your last workout. Reduce the weight only if you can't perform 10 reps with proper form. Rest 30 seconds between sets, and 1 minute between exercises, expect on bench press and military press, where you should rest 1 minute between sets, and 2 minutes between exercises.

Day 27

Jack knives   30/4

Hanging leg raises 15/3

Side plank 1 minute and 45 seconds (each side)

Running

2600m with moderate speed

Sprint 60m as fast as you can

15m as fast as you can/8

Rest 10 seconds between sets and 45 seconds between exercises on your ab workout. Go straight for the sprint after 2600m on running. Rest 2 minutes after sprint and proceed to next exercise. Rest 10 seconds between sets.

Day 28

40 minutes of running with a moderate speed

Deadlift   5/10 +2.5 kg or 10/5

Muscle ups 2/10

Chin ups with bicep focus 15/6

Add 2.5 kg to your deadlift. If you can't perform 5 reps with increased weight, double the amount of reps on one set, and increase the weight on your next workout. Focus on really squeezing your biceps on chin ups. Reduce the kip to minimum on muscle ups once you get better. Rest 45 seconds between sets and 1 minute and 15 seconds between exercises, except on deadlifts where you should rest 1 minute between sets and 2 minutes between exercises.

Day 29

"Rocky" Sprinting Stairs 20 min.

Jack knives   30/5

Hanging leg raises 15/4

Side plank 2 minutes (each side)

Plank 2 minutes

Rest 15 seconds between sets and 30 seconds between exercises on your ab workout. Rest 30 seconds between sets.

Day 30

25 minutes of running with a moderate speed

Single Leg Burpee (5 each leg) 10/3

Single Leg Plyo squat Jump 10/2

Back Squat 5/5 +2.5kg or 10/3

Leg press 10/4 +2.5kg or 20/2

Seated calf raise 15/4 +5kg

Add 2.5 kg to your back squat and leg press, and 5kg to your seated calf raise. If you can't perform most of the reps properly with increased weight, double the amount of reps on one set and increase the weight on your next workout. Rest 30 seconds between sets and 1 minute between exercises, except on back squats, where you should rest 1 minute between sets, and 1 minute and 30 seconds between exercises.

Day 31

40 minutes of running with a moderate speed

Plyometric Pushups 25/4

Bench press   5/8 +2.5kg, or   10/4

Mid cable crossovers   10/6

Military press   5/8 +2.5kg or 10/4

Close grip bench press 10/3

Add 2.5 kg to your bench press and military press. If you can't perform 5 reps properly with increased weight, double the amount of reps on one set and increase the weight on your next workout. Rest 20 seconds between sets, and 1 minute between exercises, expect on bench press, close grip bench press and military press, where you should rest 1 minute between sets, and 2 minutes between exercises

Day 32

"Rocky" Sprinting Stairs 30 min.

Jack knives   20/4

Sit ups till failure

Hanging leg raises 15/5

Hanging windshield wipers 10/4 (Alternate sides)

Medicine Ball Crunches AMRAP

Rest 20 seconds between sets and 45 seconds between all ab exercises, except sit ups. Go straight for the sit ups after your last set of jack knives, and rest 2 minutes before performing hanging leg raises.

Day 33

Yoga/ Flexibility Day

Use this day to recover from your workouts. You will warm up lightly with a 5 minute jog and proceed to stretch every muscle in your body. Hold each stretch for 30 seconds and repeat each stretch 3 times. Try to increase your flexibility with each stretch.

Or

1 hour of any kind of yoga training you would like. This will help you increase your flexibility and muscle recovery.

Day 34

Jump rope (double unders) 30 min

Jack knives   20/5

Hanging leg raises 20/3

Hanging windshield wipers 15/3 (Alternate sides)

Rest 30 seconds between sets and 45 seconds between all ab exercises. Keep your torso steady as possible on hanging leg raises and windshield wipers. Rest 30 seconds between sets.

Day 35

40 minutes of running with a moderate speed

Back Squat 5/5 +2.5kg or 10/3

Bodyweight squat 15/2

Box jumps 10/3

Seated calf raise 20/3

Single Leg Burpee (5 each leg) 10/3

Add 2.5 kg to your back squat. If you can't perform most of the reps properly with increased weight, double the amount of reps on one set and increase the weight on your next workout. Rest 20 seconds between sets and 1 minute between exercises, except on back squats, where you should rest 1 minute between sets, and 1 minute and 30 seconds between exercises

Day 36

Bench press   5/5 +2.5kg, or   10/3

Mid cable crossovers   10/6

Military press   5/3 +2.5kg or 10/2

Dumbbell front raise   12/4

Dumbbell lateral raise   12/4

Bent over lateral raise   12/4

Bench dips   20/3

Add 2.5 kg to your bench press and military press. If you can't perform 5 reps properly with increased weight, double the amount of reps on one set and increase the weight on your next workout. Rest 20 seconds between sets, and 1 minute between exercises, expect on bench press and military press, where you should rest 1 minute between sets, and 2 minutes between exercises.

Day 37

Jack knives   20/5

Push through crunches 10/1

Hanging leg raises 20/4

Hanging windshield wipers 15/4 (Alternate sides)

Running

2800m with moderate speed

Sprint 60m as fast as you can

15m as fast as you can/9

Rest 30 seconds between sets and 45 seconds between all ab exercises, except on crunches. Go straight for them after you have finished your last set of jack knives, and rest 1 minute and 45 seconds before moving on to hanging leg raises. Keep your torso steady as possible on hanging leg raises and windshield wipers. Go straight for the sprint after 2800m. Rest 2 minutes after sprint and 10 seconds between sets.

Day 38

Deadlift   5/10 +2.5 kg or 10/5

Muscle ups 4/5

Dumbbell curls 10/5   (Each arm)

Drop set of lying cable curls

Reverse barbell curls 10/5 +2.5kg 15/4

Add 2.5 kg to your deadlift and reverse barbell curls. If you can't perform most of the reps properly with increased weight, double the amount of reps on one set, and increase the weight on your next workout. Reduce the kip to minimum on muscle ups once you get better. Go straight for the drop set of lying cable curls, after you have finished your last set of dumbbell curls. Rest 25 seconds between sets and 1 minute and 30 seconds between exercises, except on deadlifts where you should rest 1 minute between sets and 2 minutes between exercises.

Day 39

"Rocky" Sprinting Stairs 15 min.

Jack knives   20/5

Push through crunches 15/1

Hanging leg raises 20/5

Hanging windshield wipers 20/3 (Alternate sides)

Rest 30 seconds between sets and 45 seconds between all ab exercises, except on crunches. Go straight for them after you have finished your last set of jack knives, and rest 1 minute and 45 seconds before moving on to hanging leg raises. Keep your torso steady as possible on hanging leg raises and windshield wipers. Rest 35 seconds between sets.

Day 40

35 minutes of running with a moderate speed

Back Squat   5/5 +2.5kg or 10/3

Leg extension   15/3

Romanian deadlift 15/4

Seated calf raise 20/4

Tuck jumps till failure

Single Leg Plyo squat Jump 20/2

Add 2.5 kg to your back squat. If you can't perform most of the reps properly with increased weight, double the amount of reps on one set and increase the weight on your next workout. Rest 30 seconds between sets and 1 minute between exercises, except on back squats, where you should rest 1 minute between sets, and 1 minute and 30 seconds between exercises.

Day 41

Yoga/ Flexibility Day

Use this day to recover from your workouts. You will warm up lightly with a 5 minute jog and proceed to stretch every muscle in your body. Hold each stretch for 30 seconds and repeat each stretch 3 times. Try to increase your flexibility with each stretch.

Or

1 hour of any kind of yoga training you would like. This will help you increase your flexibility and muscle recovery.

Day 42

Jump rope 20 min

Medicine Ball Crunches AMRAP

12 Sit ups

10 Hanging windshield wipers (Alternate sides)

10 Hanging leg raises

10 Hanging knee raises

Repeat this cycle of ab exercises for 4 times. Do not rest between exercises. Rest 2 minutes after each completed cycle. Keep your torso steady as possible on hanging leg raises, hanging knee raises and on hanging windshield wipers.

Day 43

Deadlift   5/5 +2.5 kg or 10/5

Muscle ups 5/4

Pull ups 10

Dumbbell curls 10   (Each arm)

Reverse barbell curls 10

Add 2.5 kg to your deadlift. If you can't perform most of the reps properly with increased weight, double the amount of reps on one set, and increase the weight on your next workout. Reduce the kip to minimum on muscle ups once you get better. Rest 1 minute between sets and 2 minutes between exercises on deadlifts and muscle ups. After you have finished your last set of muscle ups, rest 2 minutes, and perform this cycle of pull ups, dumbbell curls and reverse barbell curls 4 times, without resting between exercises. Rest 2 minutes after each completed cycle.

Day 44

20 minutes of running with a moderate
speed

15 Sit ups

12 Hanging windshield wipers (Alternate
sides)

12 Hanging leg raises

12 Hanging knee raises

Repeat this cycle of ab exercises for 4
times. Do not rest between exercises. Rest
2 minutes after each completed cycle.
Keep your torso steady as possible on
hanging leg raises and windshield wipers.
Rest 35 seconds between sets.

Day 45

"Rocky" Sprinting Stairs 15 min.

Back Squat   5/4 +2.5kg or 10/3
Romanian deadlift 10/4 2.5kg or 20/3

Seated calf raise   30/3

Bodyweight squats 10

Leg extension 10

Tuck jumps   10

Add 2.5 kg to your back squat and Romanian deadlift. If you can't perform most of the reps properly with increased weight, double the amount of reps in one set and increase the weight on your next workout. Rest 30 seconds between sets and 1 minute between exercises, except on back squats, where you should rest 1 minute between sets, and 1 minute and 30 seconds between exercises. After you have finished your last set of seated calf raises, go straight for the exercises below. Repeat this cycle for 3 times, and rest 2 minutes after each completed cycle.

Day 46

Bench press	5/5 +2.5kg, or 10/3
Military press	5/3 +2.5kg or 10/2
Dumbbell bench press	10
Dumbbell front raise	10
Dumbbell lateral raise	10
Bent over lateral raise	10
Bench dips	15

Add 2.5 kg to your bench press and military press. If you can't perform 5 reps properly with increased weight, double the amount of reps on one set and increase the weight on your next workout. Rest 1 minute between sets, and 2 minutes between exercises on bench press and military press. After you have finished your last set of military press, repeat this cycle below 3 times. Do not rest between exercises, and rest 2 minutes after each completed cycle.

Day 47

20 Sit ups

14 Hanging windshield wipers (Alternate sides)

14 Hanging leg raises

14 Hanging knee raises

Running

3000 m with moderate speed

Sprint 60m as fast as you can

15m as fast as you can/10

Repeat this cycle of ab exercises 3 times. Do not rest between exercises. Rest 2 minutes after each completed cycle. Keep your torso steady as possible on hanging leg raises and windshield wipers. Go straight for the sprint after 3000m. Rest 2 minutes after sprint, and 10 seconds between sets.

Day 48

Yoga/ Flexibility Day

Use this day to recover from your workouts. You will warm up lightly with a 5 minute jog and proceed to stretch every muscle in your body. Hold each stretch for 30 seconds and repeat each stretch 3 times. Try to increase your flexibility with each stretch.
Or
1 hour of any kind of yoga training you would like. This will help you increase your flexibility and muscle recovery.

Day 49

Jump rope (double unders) 20 min

25 Sit ups

16 Hanging windshield wipers (Alternate sides)

14 Hanging leg raises

16 Hanging knee raises
Medicine Ball Crunches AMRAP

Repeat this cycle of ab exercises 3 times. Do not rest between exercises. Rest 2 minutes after each completed cycle. Keep your torso steady as possible on hanging leg raises and windshield wipers. Rest 35 seconds between sets.

Day 50

35 minutes of running with a moderate speed

Back Squat   5/3 +2.5kg or 10/2

Romanian deadlift 15/4

Seated calf raise   25/4

Bodyweight squats 15

Single Leg Plyo squat Jump 18/2

Box jumps   15

Add 2.5 kg to your back squat. If you can't perform most of the reps properly with increased weight, double the amount of reps in one set and increase the weight on your next workout. Rest 30 seconds between sets and 1 minute between exercises, except on back squats, where you should rest 1 minute between sets, and 1 minute and 30 seconds between exercises. After you have finished your last set of seated calf raises, go straight for the exercises below. Repeat this cycle for 3 times, and rest 2 minutes after each completed cycle.

Day 51

"Rocky" Sprinting Stairs 15 min.

Bench press   5/4 +2.5kg, or   10/2

Military press   5/3 +2.5kg or 10/2

Dumbbell bench press 15

Dumbbell overhead press 10

Bent over lateral raise   15

Triceps pushdowns   15

Add 2.5 kg to your bench press and military press. If you can't perform 5 reps properly with increased weight, double the amount of reps on one set and increase the weight on your next workout. Rest 1 minute between sets, and 2 minutes between exercises on bench press and military press. After you have finished your last set of military press, repeat this cycle below 3 times.

Day 52

Jump rope (double unders) 20 min

25 Sit ups

18 Hanging windshield wipers (Alternate sides)

16 Hanging leg raises

18 Hanging knee raises

Medicine Ball Crunches AMRAP

Repeat this cycle of ab exercises 3 times. Do not rest between exercises. Rest 2 minutes after each completed cycle. Keep your torso steady as possible on hanging leg raises and windshield wipers.

Day 53

Yoga/ Flexibility Day

Use this day to recover from your workouts. You will warm up lightly with a 5 minute jog and proceed to stretch every muscle in your body. Hold each stretch for 30 seconds and repeat each stretch 3 times. Try to increase your flexibility with each stretch.

Or

1 hour of any kind of yoga training you would like. This will help you increase your flexibility and muscle recovery.

Day 54

"Rocky" Sprinting Stairs 20 min.

25 Sit ups

18 Hanging windshield wipers (Alternate sides)

16 Hanging leg raises

18 Hanging knee raises

Repeat this cycle of ab exercises for 4 times. Do not rest between exercises. Rest 2 minutes after each completed cycle. Keep your torso steady as possible on hanging leg raises, hanging knee raises, and on hanging windshield wipers. Rest 45 seconds between sets.

Day 55

35 minutes of running with a moderate speed

Back Squat   5/3 +2.5kg or 10/2

Romanian deadlift 10/3 +2.5kg, or 20/4

Seated calf raise   15/3

Leg press   10

Bodyweight squats 15

Bodyweight lunges   10 (Alternate legs)

Add 2.5 kg to your back squat and romanian deadlift, and 5kg to your seated calf raise. If you can't perform most of the reps properly with increased weight, double the amount of reps in one set and increase the weight on your next workout. Rest 30 seconds between sets and 1 minute between exercises, except on back squats, where you should rest 1 minute between sets, and 1 minute and 30 seconds between exercises. After you have finished your last set of seated calf raises, go straight for the exercises below. Repeat this cycle for 4 times, and rest 2 minutes after each completed cycle.

Day 56

Jump rope (double unders) 15 min

Handstand Wall Walks 6/3

Bench press   5/5 +2.5kg, or   10/3

Weighted dips with chest focus   15/2

Dumbbell overhead press   15/4

Bent over lateral raise   10/4 with heavier
dbs, or 20/3

Skullcrushers   12/5
Add 2.5 kg to your bench press. If you
can't perform 5 reps properly with
increased weight, double the amount of
reps on one set and increase the weight on
your next workout. Switch to heavier dbs
on bent over lateral raises, or do as
instructed and increase the weight on your
next workout. Rest 30 seconds between
sets and 1 minute between exercises,
except on bench press, where you should
rest 1 minute between sets, and 2 minutes
between exercises.

Day 57

25/2 Sit ups

20/2 Hanging windshield wipers (Alternate sides)

18/2 Hanging leg raises

20/2 Hanging knee raises

Running
3200m with moderate speed

Sprint 60m as fast as you can

15m as fast as you can/11

Repeat this cycle of ab exercises 2 times. Rest 20 seconds between sets and exercises, and 1 minute after each cycle. Keep your torso steady as possible on hanging leg raises, hanging knee raises, and on hanging windshield wipers. Go straight for the sprint after 3200m. Rest 2 minutes after sprint and 10 seconds between sets.

Day 58

"Rocky" Sprinting Stairs 20 min.

Deadlift   5 +2.5 kg or 10

Dumbbell rows 10 (Each side)
Pull ups   15
Barbell curls   10/4 +2.5kg, or 20/3
Drop set of lying cable curls
Reverse barbell curls   15/5

Add 2.5 kg to your deadlift and barbell curls. If you can't perform most of the reps properly with increased weight, double the amount of reps on one set, and increase the weight on your next workout. Repeat this cycle of back exercises 4 times. Do not rest between exercises and rest 2 minutes after each completed cycle. After you have finished your back exercises, go for the bicep workout below. Dropset means that once you have reached muscle failure with heavier weight, you reduce the weight and keep doing more repetitions until you reach muscle failure again. Rest 20 seconds between sets and 30 seconds between exercises on your bicep workout.

Day 59

Jump rope (double unders) 30 min

Medicine Ball Crunches AMRAP

30/2 Sit ups

25/2 Hanging windshield wipers (Alternate sides)

25/2 Hanging leg raises

Repeat this cycle of ab exercises for 2 times. Rest 20 seconds between sets and exercises, and 1 minute after each cycle. Keep your torso steady as possible on hanging leg raises, hanging knee raises, and on hanging windshield wipers. Rest 45 seconds between sets.

Day 60

Yoga/ Flexibility Day

Use this day to recover from your workouts. You will warm up lightly with a 5 minute jog and proceed to stretch every muscle in your body. Hold each stretch for 30 seconds and repeat each stretch 3 times. Try to increase your flexibility with each stretch.

Or

1 hour of any kind of yoga training you would like. This will help you increase your flexibility and muscle recovery.

Chapter 5:
Rest to be the Best

"Rest is the golden chain that ties health and our bodies together." Dekker

During the past couple of years studies have been done to seek ways to improve overall performance. Proper recovery has proven to aid in the restoration of physiological and psychological processes, so that the athlete can compete or train again at a high performance level.

Training or competing at high levels of intensity will speed up their metabolism, push their central nervous system, exhaust the muscles of their body, alter their emotional state, and increase their body temperature. The strain from exercise is great but not allowing your body to properly recuperate will lead to injury, reduced performance, and burnout.

Overtraining is a big concern for athletes who train every day of the week. You might start off on a good track, but too much exercise isn't actually a good thing because your body requires rest in order to get stronger and to rebuild itself. One day of active recovery between workout sessions for a beginner is ok, but this all depends on each individual's ability to recover. If you answer yes to one more of the following questions chances are you are overtraining.

Are you moody? Do you have trouble sleeping? You don't feel like eating? Your resting heart rate is very high?
If you don't watch it, you are going to end up with overuse injuries.

Rest and recovery are essential in having your body healthy. At least one day a week must be dedicated to rest and recovery. Allowing your body to recover is part of your training, which is why we need to understand what must be done in this period.
Recovery should be an active process that is a part of the complete training program.

The conditions of the training must be taken into account when preparing a recovery plan. For example:

- Training and competition. Volume, intensity, duration of exercise, fatigue levels and previous recovery periods.

- Environment. Humidity and temperature.
- Nutrition. Amount of nutrients and hydration level depleted.
- Lifestyle. Quality of sleep, schedule and social activities.
- Psychological. The stress and tension from competing.
- Health. Previous injuries or illness.

Immediate, Short and Long Term Recovery

Not all recovery should be the same, the amount of time that has passed since the exercise is important to consider. There are three categories of recovery. There is immediate or short term recovery from an intense training session or competition, and there is the long term recovery that needs to be incorporated into a training schedule. Each is extremely important for ideal sports performance.

Immediate recovery

Immediate recovery must take place within the first thirty minutes after competition or training. This recovery could also be considered as a cool down mentioned previously, a time for lowering body temperature and heart rate and stretching.

Another focus of recovery immediately following exercise has to do with refueling energy reserves and rehydrating what was lost during exercise by eating the right foods and drinks.

Research has shown that the window for ideal recovery is slim, ideally within 15-60 minutes after completing the last exercise your focus must be to refuel and rehydrate.

To refuel it's best to consume a fruit, protein shake, energy bar, or sports drink immediately following a competition or intense training. Do this before anything else. The nourishment you choose should provide about 0.8 gram of carbs per kilogram of body weight and 0.4 gram of protein per kilogram of body weight.

Following training, or competition, your body is left dehydrated, low on fuel, and energy. Your body is in a strained state, and the proper combination of nutrients can boost the body's recovery process to help you come back stronger and healthier.

To rehydrate try to measure how many pounds of sweat were lost during training or competition. For every pound lost you must replenish it with 20-24 oz. of water. I understand it's not always easy to travel around with a scale but it does help to be more precise. Another way to check the rehydration levels is in your urine. The darker the urine the more dehydrated you are, the clearer the urine the better hydrated you are.

Electrolytes are also lost in sweat. Minerals such as potassium and sodium are needed to help the body perform normally, and they can be easily substituted by the foods and fluids you eat after a workout or an event. A banana for example is high in potassium. For the lost sodium, sports drinks or electrolyte water can help recover lost minerals as can sodium heavy foods.

Short term recovery

Short term recovery takes place within 24 – 48 hours after an intense training or competition. It's essentially a day of light exercise, with some stretching or form drills. The primary goal of the short term recovery is to increase circulation to bring oxygen rich blood to recovering tissues and aid in returning muscles to normal tension and size.

An example of a short term recovery day would be calm 20-30 minutes of light aerobic exercise being a stationary bicycle, jogging or light lifting. Followed by static stretching and self-massage with a foam roller. The muscles are now ready for a hot or cold shower.

Your body is now better prepared mentally and physically for the next day's training or competition.

Long Term Recovery

Long term recovery must be incorporated into every athlete's training schedule. This recovery is scheduled by the coach or yourself. During a season there are several spikes in intensity and training. Before competition there would be a spike in training intensity in order to prepare for the event. After the event there would come a decrease in intensity. This decrease would be considered long term recovery. A specific portion of the season is designated to recovery. The duration of long term recovery would depend on the intensity of the season and the upcoming events.

Here are some tips for adding rest and recovery to your routine:

1)   Develop a configuration of training of "intense day, easy day"

2)   If you have a long day at work or difficult obligations ahead, schedule a recovery day

 3)   If you are engaged in several sports beware: Don't turn the fact that you can train several different sports into an excuse to go hard almost every day.

4)   When in doubt, go for a short term recovery day

Sleep

After working so hard your mind and body must rest. Many decide to stay up late watching TV. or on the computer thinking that this is relaxation time. But, if you are awake it doesn't count. Your body and mind need to enter in a shutdown mode. Your deep breathing helps relax your muscles and your mind disengages from all stress and anxiety.

There is no substitute for a good night rest. Top athletes claim they simply cannot perform at their peak unless they have a good 10-12 hours of sleep every night.

Sleep is equally as important as exercise and nutrition to any athlete who wishes to be successful. Any high performance athlete understands they make a living from their body's performance. The detrimental effects of not enough sleep are the same for athletes as anyone else: decrease in stamina, attention, reaction, strength, and alertness. These are all skills required to perform at an elite level.

Why is sleep so important for athletes?

It has a lot to do with recovery. Recuperation increases your energy levels, enhances your immune system, and allows you get the most out of each training session, which in the end will improve your performance.

Athletes nowadays are training harder than ever, completing the right amount of sleep is extremely important to recovery. With each practice or competition stress is placed on the mind, the body and muscle tissue is worn out with energy levels being exhausted. While you sleep the body releases potent growth hormones which are in charge of muscle repair and growth.

Their body needs a certain amount of time spent in deep sleep to reconstruct and repair tissues. If it is allowed to complete this task each night without interruption, then their body is best prepared for the next day of training or competition.

Are you sleeping the right amount of hours?

Do not allow yourself to waste these precious hours of improving and recovery playing video games, watching television or on the computer! Your body and mind need to shut down, develop, grow and recover.

Improving Sleep

As we have read above sleep is crucial in order to perform at the highest levels. In order to catch the perfect zzz's there are several tips to follow.

1) Get on a schedule. Go to bed and wake up at a similar time every day.

2) Keep the room dark. Low light is soothing and relaxes the mind.

3) Cool temperatures. Your body temperature tracks your circadian rhythm. If you are in a warm environment your circadian rhythm will have difficulty decreasing.

4) Background noise. The main reason for waking up are intrusive noise events such as dog barking

or door pounding. To blend these noises background noise is suggested such as a fan or sound machine.

5) Keep it comfortable. If you have a pillow that you like, or a blanket that soothes you use it. Stay comfortable with a loose pajama and a relaxed surrounding.

Treat sleep like a secret weapon. Go to sleep and wake up a better athlete overnight. Start sleeping more and you'll become a better athlete setting new personal records. Get healthier, happier and fitter by sleeping more.

By taking care of your body you can enjoy your sports at your highest level of performance and in a healthy disposition.

Chapter 6:
Eat your way to success

"Take care of your body, it's the only place we have to live. " Jim Rohn

Could eating a right meal make a difference in your performance? Of course!
Feeding your body properly is crucial to performing at a top level. Your body runs on whatever you feed it. Your meals are your fuel. If you want your body to performance at its full potential, you must keep it perfectly fine tuned.
When feeding yourself it's important to educate yourself about the meals you are eating, and how will this benefit your body. Ideally you would like to have a healthy, well rounded and complete diet. Remember these healthy habits you are instilling will carry on throughout your life. Later on you will be very proud of what you have accomplished.

RMR

We all have a RMR or Rest Metabolic Rate this would be the amount of calories or energy your body requires during the resting stage. This allows the body to fulfill the basic requirements the body needs to function properly. Calories are required to complete the essential body functions such as respiration, digestion, or heartbeat. Approximately 50 to 75% of an individual's daily energy requirements are credited towards the resting metabolic rate. Athletes tend to have a higher RMR because more calories are required to maintain lean body mass. To calculate the exact RMR you would need your exact height, age, weight and gender.

It's also very important to take into account the amount of hours the athlete is training. The more hours of training, the more calories would need to be consumed.

It is important to eat a variety of colorful foods that provide vitamins, minerals and antioxidants to nourish your body. For example, corn (yellow), spinach (green), sweet potato or brown rice (orange), and an apple (red). A variety of vitamins and minerals like vitamin A, vitamin C, potassium, and calcium are included in this plate. The chicken and the spinach contain protein and iron. The apple and sweet potato provide healthy carbohydrates.

It is a balance of nutrients that keeps athletes healthy and able to train hard for each session. Keep your future champion body healthy by choosing a variety of foods and keeping your plate colorful.

We mentioned above the more lean muscle the more calories need to be consumed calories due to faster metabolism. But we must provide our body with healthy calories, not empty calories. In this chapter we'll go over what are the essential meals for your body.
First, let's break down our food pyramid and discuss what foods are the essential building blocks for your body.

Protein

They are often called the building blocks of the body. Protein consists of a combination of structures called amino acids that combine in several ways to help create muscles, bone, tendons, skin, hair, and other tissues. Athletes need protein to assist in repairing and rebuilding muscle that was broken down during exercise. It also helps to optimize carbohydrate storage in the form of glycogen. Some examples of foods that contain protein are meat, poultry, fish, dairy products, eggs, soy, legumes, lentil, beans, nuts and several vegetables such as avocado, cauliflower, asparagus, broccoli and artichoke.

It's important to consider that although many red meat sources may be high in protein, they are high in saturated fats which are not healthy. Fish and poultry are a much healthier choice as a meat source protein.

Carbohydrates

They are the most important source of energy for athletes. No matter what sport you play, carbs provide the energy that fuels muscle contractions. Once carbs are consumed, they breakdown into smaller sugars that get absorbed and used as energy. A steady supply of carbohydrate intake prevents protein from being used as energy. If the body does not have enough carbohydrate, protein is broken down to create glucose for energy. This leads to weakened muscles which could lead to injuries.

Carbohydrates are both simple and complex. Simple carbohydrates have a smaller structure with only 1 or 2 sugar molecules. Some simple carbohydrates include sucrose, sugar found in candy, soda, juice. They are the fastest source of energy, as they are quickly digested, but only last for a short period of time. They tend to have little or no vitamins and minerals.

Complex carbohydrates are made of many sugar molecules looped together like a necklace. They are commonly rich in fiber, and health promoting. Complex carbohydrates are usually found in whole plant foods and, hence, are also often full of vitamins and minerals. Examples would be whole grain pasta, and wheat bread, green vegetables, peas, sweet potatoes, pumpkin and other starchy vegetables.

Healthy Fats

They are critical nutrients for optimal health. Omega-3 and Omega-6 fatty acids are required for normal growth and development and for the standard functioning of the brain and nervous system. Fat is the main fuel source for low-level to modest exercise such as walking or jogging, and is very important for extended endurance trials that are at lower intensities. While fat is easily deposited in the body and is calorie-dense, it also takes longer to breakdown and digest. It can take up to 6 hours to be converted into a usable form of energy. This would clearly identify fat unsuitable as a pre- exercise snack.

When consuming, choose "good fats" such as polyunsaturated and monounsaturated fats which are found in fish, nuts, seeds, canola and olive oils, flax seeds and avocados.

Limit consumption of foods with "bad fats" such as butter, potato chips, pizza, bacon, ribs or any solid fat. They contain trans fats and saturated fats. Too much of these have been linked to health problems such as high cholesterol, heart disease and poor athletic performance.

Nutrition Numbers for Champions

The distribution of nutrients recommended for athletes are as follows.

Protein: Assists muscle recovery when consumed after exercising and should represent 10% to 15% of calories. Recommendations for total protein consumptions are at least 0.95 grams per kilogram per day

Carbohydrates: **Are** the most vital source of energy for an athlete and should account for 55% of calories or even more on intense exercising days. Recommendations for daily consumption are approximately 5 to 8 grams per kilogram of body weight.

Fats: Should represent 25% to 30% of total calories. High-fat foods must be avoided as they can cause uneasiness if eaten too close to the start of physical activity. Limit consumption of trans fats and saturated fats. Emphasize healthy fats that are found in avocados, tuna, canola oil, soy, and nuts.

Vitamins and Minerals

Vitamins are vital elements that must be consumed because the body does not produce them by itself. They are essential to maintain healthy and balanced body functions.

Fruits and vegetables contain vitamins, minerals and antioxidants that are essential to maintaining a healthy and balanced diet. Examples are: Oranges, a great source for vitamin c, bananas for potassium, and carrots for beta carotene.

Two important minerals to consider in athletes are Calcium and Iron. Calcium helps build stronger bones, which decreases the chance of them breaking under stress or heavy activity. You can find calcium in many dairy products, such as milk, yogurt, and cheese. Also include dark, green leafy vegetables and calcium-fortified products, like orange juice as good sources of calcium.

Now we'll go into to detail into several important vitamins and minerals and better understand how they help us and where we can find them.

Vitamin A

Well known for proper vision development, it also has many other benefits. It maintains red and white blood cell production and activity. Promotes a healthy immune system, and keep skin healthy.

An optimal daily intake for a male would be 900 micrograms and for a female would be 700 micrograms.

Good sources of Vitamin A are eggs, milk, liver and giblets, cod liver oil, squash, sweet potato, carrots, kale, apricot, peaches, cantaloupe, papaya, and mango.

In order to reach your optimal daily these foods contain a good amount of Vitamin A. It's important to remember that many vegetables loose many vitamins and nutrients when cooked.

Cod liver oil 1 teaspoon = 1350 mcg

Kale ½ cup = 443 mcg

Carrots ½ cup = 538 mcg

Cantaloupe ½ melon = 467 mcg

Spinach ½ cup = 573 mcg

Sweet Potato ½ cup = 961 mcg

Vitamin C

Vitamin C is essential for the biosynthesis of collagen. Collagen is the main protein used as connective tissue in the body. Collagen is especially important for healthy joints, ligaments, and bones. Other benefits of vitamin C include a boost in the immune system, supports in wound healing and improves brain function.

An optimal daily intake for a male or female would be 45 to 75 micrograms.

Good sources of Vitamin C are citrus fruits, leafy greens, peppers, potatoes, and cauliflower.

In order to reach your optimal daily these foods contain a good amount of Vitamin C.

Red pepper raw ½ cup = 95 mcg

Orange juice ¾ cup = 93 mcg

Broccoli cooked ½ cup = 51 mcg

Kiwi fruit = 64 mcg

Strawberries ½ cup = 49 mcg

Vitamin D

Vitamin D is vital for proper calcium metabolism. Bone density is linked directly to this vitamin, as well as a good nervous system function and immunity.

This vitamin is a special one, it allows your body to manufacture Vitamin D when you get sunlight on your skin. No need to bask in the sunlight, no more than few minutes a day are required.

Vitamin D is not easily found in food in nature, which is why many products are now fortified with this Vitamin. Such as milk, yogurt, and fortified cereals.

An optimal daily intake for a male or female would be 15 mcg.

Good sources of Vitamin D are:

Fortified milk 1 cup = 2.4 mcg

Salmon 3 oz. = 13 mcg

Egg yolk 1 = 0.5 mcg

Vitamin E

Vitamin E is also called the excellent vitamin. It pertains to a family of eight antioxidants and as such protects our bodies from damage. Constantly battling free radicals protects essential lipids and maintains the balance of cell membranes. Naturally an anti-inflammatory, it aids in muscle wellness.

An optimal daily intake for a male or female would be15 micrograms.

Good sources of Vitamin E are nuts, seeds, avocado, wheat grains, and oils.

In order to reach your optimal daily these foods contain a good amount of Vitamin E.

Wheat germ oil 1 tablespoon = 20 mcg

Sunflower seeds 1 ounce = 7.4 mcg

Peanut butter 2 tablespoons = 2.9 mcg

Almonds roasted 1 ounce = 6.8 mcg

Vitamin K

The K in vitamin K is from German origin for "Koagulation" which means coagulation in German. This vitamin is essential for coagulation in our bodies. Deficiencies are visible with easy bruising, nosebleeds, and heavy menstrual periods.

An optimal daily intake for a male would be 80 mcg or female would be 65 micrograms.

Vitamin K is readily available in many foods we eat day to day, but is especially concentrated in leafy greens.

Kale ½ cup = 531 mcg

Spinach ½ cup = 444 mcg

Broccoli 1 cup = 220 mcg

Swiss Chard 1 cup = 290 mcg

Minerals

Minerals are nutrients your body requires to function properly. They are consumed mostly in animal and plant form. Without these minerals we would be prone to illness, and a lack of performance.

Zinc

Zinc is a trace element that is found in natural foods, fortified foods and as a dietary supplement. It aids in the breakdown of protein, fat and carbohydrates. It also assists in wound healing and immune wellbeing. Zinc deficiency is dangerous because it supports proper growth and development of the body.

An optimal daily intake for a male and female would be 8 to 11 micrograms.

Zinc is readily available in many foods we eat day to day such as seafood, chicken, fortified cereals, and beef.

Lobster 3 ounces = 3.4 mcg

Chicken 3 ounces = 2.4 mcg

Fortified cereal ¾ cup = 3.8 mcg

Potassium

This mineral and electrolyte is important enough to make our heart beat. Yes, its functions include the transmission of nervous system signals, muscle movement, and a steady heartbeat. Potassium also lowers blood pressure and also helps our bones.

This mineral is essential to any athlete any deficiency leads to muscle cramping, vomiting and fatigue.

An optimal daily intake for a male and female would be approximately 2000 mg.

Many sports drinks include potassium, and we often see athletes eating a banana or two which also contains potassium. But these foods are also good sources:

Plums ½ cup = 637 mg

Baked Potatoes = 926 mg

Raisins ½ cup = 598 mg

Banana = 422 mg

Iron

Iron is essential for growth, development, synthesis of several hormones, and normal functioning. But it's most important function is to help hemoglobin and myoglobin (components of red blood cells and muscles) bring oxygen to all the cells that require it.

This mineral is easiest absorbed through red meat and poultry. It is recommended for vegetarians to consume iron rich foods or dietary supplements.

An optimal daily intake for a male would be 8 mg. and female would be 15 mg.

The following are excellent sources of iron:

Beef cooked 6 ounces = 4.64 mg

Cooked lentils ½ cup = 3.30 mg

Spinach boiled ½ cup = 3 mg

Tofu ½ cup = 3 mg

Calcium

Calcium is probably the most talked about mineral and the most abundant mineral in our bodies. Since we are little kids we are constantly reminded to drink milk for strong bones and teeth. Most dairy products contain high amounts of calcium.

Calcium is crucial for the wellbeing of bones, teeth, and muscle contraction. A deficiency in this vitamin will cause poor teeth and brittle bones.

An optimal daily intake for a male and female would be 1300 mg.

Good sources of calcium are:

Yogurt plain 8 ounces = 415 mg

Kale raw 1 cup = 100 mg

Whole Milk 8 ounces = 276 mg

Mozzarella Cheese 2 ounces = 335 mg

Magnesium

Magnesium is a mineral that collaborates with calcium to help with proper muscle contraction, energy metabolism, blood clotting, and building healthy teeth and bones.

Magnesium is widely available in plants and animal foods. An optimal daily intake for an male would be 240-400 mg or female would be 250-350 mg

Good sources of magnesium are:

Brazil nuts 1 ounce = 107 mg

Pumpkin 1 ounce = 151 mg

Banana = 44 mg

Dietary Supplements

In order to maintain your body healthy and at its peak a balanced diet is required. But to avoid any deficiency in vitamins and minerals a dietary supplement is recommended. These are not a substitute for a healthy diet or to cure any medical conditions. We would consider them as a backup, to complete the requirements of any missing vitamins or minerals in our diet.

These are easily available in pharmacies and supermarkets. It's important to keep in mind what exactly you're missing before administering these supplements. Please be mindful and follow the instructions on the labels.

Extra tips

Include foods rich in iron in your diet, like meat, dried beans, and fortified cereals. With a decreased iron diet, energy levels in athletes decrease. Females who have their menstrual cycle lose iron every month. Another way many minerals are lost is through their sweat.

Consider each meal a **colorful one**. Aim for at least 4 or more colors, such as: carrots (orange) 1, spinach (green) 2, tomato (red) 3, pasta (white) 4, grass fed beef (brown) 5. The more colors, the more nutrients your body is acquiring.

It's also important to consider the individual needs for each individual. Age, gender, and size also are factors to consider. Every individual will require a different amount of calories. What remains fixed is a healthy and balanced meal for each as mentioned above.

Now that we can properly differentiate the values of each type of food, it's important to understand when the best time to consume each is.

Before a workout

Remain with foods that you are familiar with.

Three to four hours before your workout is the ideal time to have a meal. The meal should be high in carbohydrates, moderate in lean protein and low in fats. An example would be whole wheat pasta, with grilled chicken and a salad.

One to two hours before your workout a small snack is recommended to avoid hunger and maintain high energy levels. An example would be a bagel, banana or other fruit.

During a workout

Fruits like banana and oranges are recommended. Nothing substantial should be consumed to avoid feeling sluggish and heavy.

Water and sports drinks also help maintain optimal energy levels.

After a workout

Ideally within one to two hours after a workout, a meal should be consumed that is high in protein and high in carbohydrates. The longer an athlete takes to consume this recovery meal, the longer it takes to replenish the energy lost. The main goal is to replenish and recuperate the body.

Avoid at all times

We must have the same discipline in training as we do in our nutrition. Many of the following foods can be eaten on a rare occasion, but they should not be considered a snack or part of an everyday diet.

Foods like chips, Cheetos, sweets, cakes, cookies, carbonated sodas, fast foods, artificial colors, high fructose corn syrup, preservatives and empty calorie snacks. They will hinder performance and decrease overall good health.

Remember: **When you think you're done training, you're not done training, at least not until you've put some nutrients back into your body.**

Just as important as your workout is what you do as soon as you finish your workout. If you forget to nourish your body, you'll never get the full worth out of all the work you just put in… and what a waste that would be.

Your best performance simply won't happen if you lose focus on your body's needs for nutrients. Give your body what it needs immediately after exercising, when it's most receptive to replenishment, and it will respond wonderfully.

Chapter 7
PALEO Recipes

"You don't have to cook fancy or complicated masterpieces – just good food from fresh ingredients." Julia Child

These are several of my favorite recipes that I am sharing with you, feel free to adapt and expand these recipes with other paleo foods. Be creative with your meals, mix and match foods. Think of your favorite meals and combine them into something great. Try new foods you've never tried before, you might be surprised.

Nature provides us with so much variety with textures, flavors and colors, we are extremely lucky to be able to enjoy it all.

In this chapter you will find a total of 50 recipes: 10 for breakfast, 10 for lunch, 10 for dinner, 10 for snacks and 10 for dessert.

I hope you enjoy them all!

Breakfast

1. Fresh fruit salad with mint and honey dressing
(8 servings)

Ingredients
- 4 cups peeled and cubed watermelon
- 2 cups fresh strawberries
- 2 large oranges cut into cubes
- 1 cup grapes seedless cut in half
- 1 large apple cut into cubes
- 1 peach cut into cubes
- Fresh lemon juice (desired amount)
- ¼ cup fresh mint leaves
- 1 tablespoon lemon zest
- 1 tablespoon honey

Directions

Place all the fruit in a large bowl.
In a smaller bowl whisk lemon juice, mint leaves, lemon zest and honey. Drizzle as desired over the fruit and toss to coat. Refrigerate 1 hour before serving.

2. Healthy and Delicious Banana Walnut Pancakes

(Approximately 12 servings depending on the size of the pancake)

Ingredients

- 6 large ripe bananas
- 1 tablespoon coconut oil
- 6 eggs
- 1 teaspoon coconut oil
- 2 tablespoons vanilla extract
- ½ teaspoon baking soda
- 1 teaspoon ground cinnamon
- ½ cup walnuts

Directions

Heat 1 teaspoon of coconut oil on a skillet to a medium heat. In a separate bowl mash the bananas, as they become smooth you may begin to mix in the eggs, vanilla extract, coconut oil, baking soda, vanilla extract and walnuts. Once the mixture is well combined you may cook in the skillet, cook until the edges are dry and bubbles form. This can take around 3-4 minutes. Flip and repeat on the other side.
Once it's cooked you may dust with some cinnamon, more nuts, or some fresh fruits such as strawberries or blueberries.

3. Strawberry and Banana Protein Shake
Serves 1-2

Ingredients

- 1 large frozen banana
- 1 cup frozen strawberries
- 1 cup almond milk
- 1 scoop vanilla protein powder
- ½ vanilla extract
- 1 tablespoon ground chia seeds

Directions

Place all the ingredients in the blender.
Blend. Enjoy!

4. Green Omelet
Serves 3-4

Ingredients
- 1 cup kale
- 1 cup spinach
- ½ cup broccoli
- ½ fresh mushrooms
- 8 eggs
- ½ teaspoon coconut oil

Directions

Begin by heating the skillet at medium to high heat with coconut oil.
Chop your kale, spinach, broccoli, and mushrooms into bite sized pieces. In a separate bowl open the eggs and whisk until uniform. Place the vegetables in the skillet and immediately place the eggs in the skillet. Allow to cook until eggs no longer are runny. This will take around 8 minutes. You may sprinkle some salt or pepper as desired.

5. Baked Avocado with Eggs
2 servings

Ingredients

- 1 large avocado cut in half and pitted
- 2 eggs
- 25 grams prosciutto
- 1 tablespoon basil

Directions

Preheat oven to 425 degrees Fahrenheit or 220 Celsius. Place the avocados in a baking dish making sure they are facing up.
Open one egg and place inside the avocado, repeat the process with the second avocado half.
Gently place the baking dish in the oven and allow to cook for 15 minutes.
Remove from the oven and garnish with the prosciutto and basil.

6. Green Smoothie
1-2 serving

Ingredients

- ½ cup almond milk
- ½ cup strawberries
- 1 cup packed spinach
- 1 large banana
- ½ avocado
- 3 tablespoons
- ½ cup ice (if you like it cold)

Directions
Place all ingredients in the blender. Blend.
Enjoy!

7. Almond Muffins

4 servings

Ingredients

- 1 cup blanched almond flour
- 2 large eggs
- 1 tablespoon honey
- ¼ teaspoon baking soda
- ½ teaspoon apple cider vinegar
- Optional raisins, cranberries, almond slivers

Directions

Preheat oven to 350 degrees Fahrenheit. In a bowl combine almond flour and baking soda. In a separate bowl combine the eggs, honey and vinegar. Gently mix dry ingredients into wet bowl, mixing well until combined. You may mix in your choice of almond slivers, cranberries or raisins. Place in muffin pan and bake for 15 minutes or until slightly brown around the edges.
Allow to cool for 15 minutes before serving.

8. Power Up Smoothie
1-2 servings

Ingredients
- Avocado peeled and pitted
- ½ banana fresh or frozen
- 1 peach fresh
- ½ cup kale
- 1 cup coconut milk

Directions
Place all the ingredients in the blender.
Blend. Enjoy!

9. Quick Banana Bites
Serves 1

Ingredients

- 1 large banana
- 4 tablespoons Almond butter

Directions
Peel and slice your banana into an even amount of round slices about 0.5 inches thick. Spread a desired amount of almond butter on each slice. Place together 2 slices as a sandwich.

You may place in the freezer for 10 minutes or eat right away.

10. Berries and Cream

Serves 2

Ingredients

- 2 cups fresh mixed berries
  (blackberries, strawberries, blueberries
  or raspberries)
- 1 can coconut milk
- 1 tablespoon honey

Directions

Place can of coconut milk for a minimum of
5 hours or overnight. When you open the
can scoop the heavy cream that has risen
to the top of the container. Place in a bowl
and whisk until fluffy.
Place the cream on top of the berries.
Gently drizzle the honey on top of both the
cream and honey. Feel free to add some
mint to garnish.

Lunch

1. Paleo Spanish Clams
Serves 2-3

Ingredients

- 2 lbs. washed clams
- 1 cup fresh cilantro finely chopped
- 1 clove garlic finely chopped
- 1 tablespoon lemon
- ¼ cup coconut oil
- ½ cup white wine
- Salt as desired
- ½ cup water

Directions
Make sure you wash the clams in cold water to remove any remaining salt or sediment. Place the water, oil, wine and garlic and bring to boil. Add the clams and cilantro. Stir frequently for 5-10 minutes. The clams are ready when the shells open and the meat in tender-firm. Serve immediately.

2. Hearty Lamb Roast
Serves 3-4

Ingredients

- 1 lb. lamb stew meat cubed
- 4 tomatoes cubed
- 1 onion chopped
- 2 garlic cloves
- 2 cups mushrooms halved
- 3 carrots peels and chopped
- 2 tablespoons rosemary
- 2 cups water
- Salt and Pepper as desired

Directions

Preheat oven to 325 degrees Fahrenheit.
In a large baking dish place the tomatoes,
mushrooms, carrots, onions and garlic.
Add the lamb, rosemary, water, and salt
and pepper.
Mix well and place in the oven for about 2
hours, stirring every 30-40 minutes. When
the lamb is very tender, and a light brown
color it's ready to be served.

3. Grilled Rosemary Lemon Chicken
Serves 1-2

Ingredients

- 1 lb skinless, boneless chicken breast
- 2 tablespoons olive oil
- ¼ cup lemon juice
- 1 garlic clove finely chopped
- ¼ fresh rosemary minced
- Salt as desired

Directions

In a small bowl combine lemon juice, olive oil, rosemary and salt. Place chicken in baking dish. Pour marinade over chicken, cover and refrigerate anywhere from 20 minutes to 6 hours. Heat the grill and cook chicken 7-8 minutes per side or until browned and cooked in the center. Serve immediately.

4. Cod Mediterranean Delight
Serves 4-6

Ingredients

- 1 ½ lbs. cod
- ½ blanched almond flour
- 5 tablespoons olive oil
- 5 tablespoons grape seed oil
- 1/2 cup water
- ¼ cup lemon juice
- ¼ brined capers
- ¼ cup parsley chopped

Directions

Cut cod into 4 pieces. Mix together flour and salt in a separate plate. Coat each cod with the flour and salt mixture, until well covered. Heat the olive oil and only 2 tablespoons of grape seed oil in a large skillet on medium to high heat. Add the cod pieces and cook until brown, 3-4 minutes per side. Transfer to plate and cover to keep warm. Add the water, lemon juice and capers to skillet and bring to boil. Add the remaining grape seed oil and whisk together. Serve the cod on a plate and pour the sauce lightly over it and sprinkle with parsley.

5. Grass Fed Rib eye Steak Stir-fry
Serves 4-6

Ingredients

- 2 pounds grass fed rib eye steak
- ½ cup onions
- ½ cup mushrooms
- ½ cup kale
- ½ cup carrots
- 1 garlic glove finely chopped
- ½ cup tomato
- ½ cup zucchini
- ½ cup yellow squash
- 1 tablespoon grape seed oil

Directions

Cut steak into cubes. Place salt and pepper as desired. Place ½ tablespoon grape seed oil on skillet on medium to high heat. Place the steak, cook until brown. Remove from heat and place all the vegetables in the skillet with ½ tablespoon grape seed oil for 3-4 minutes. Mix the steak in with the vegetables for 1 minute on the skillet at low heat. Remove from heat and allow 5 minutes for the steak to absorb all the juices then serve.

6. Savory Eggplant and Sausage
Serves 4-6

Ingredients

- 2 large eggplants cubed
- 4 sweet potatoes cubes
- 3 shallots finely chopped
- ½ cup olive oil
- 6 Italian sausage link

Directions
Preheat oven to 400 degrees Fahrenheit. Place all the ingredients in a baking dish and mix well. Bake for 30 minutes until the sausage is cooked and the eggplant is golden. Remove from oven and serve warm.

7. Chicken Soup
Serves 3-4

Ingredients

- 6 cups water
- 4 skinless chicken thighs
- ½ onion finely chopped
- ½ cup carrots cubed
- ½ cup kale
- ½ cup broccoli
- ½ cup zucchini
- Salt as desired

Directions
Place the water in a pan and begin to boil.
As soon as water boils add chicken,
onions, carrots, kale, broccoli, and
zucchini. Add salt as desired.
Boil for 30 minutes. Allow to cool 5 minutes
before serving.

8. Wild Salmon with Fresh Spinach
Serves 4

Ingredients

- 4 wild caught salmon steaks
- 3 tablespoons olive oil
- ¼ cup lemon juice
- 1 garlic clove finely chopped
- 1 teaspoon dill finely chopped
- 3 cups fresh spinach

Directions
Heat the skillet with the olive oil on a medium to high heat. Combine the lemon juice, garlic, and dill together in a bowl. Brush this combination on the salmon steaks. Place the steaks on the skillet and cook until brown on both sides. Once the salmon is cooked add the spinach, cook no more than 1-2 minutes, until the leaves look bright green. Remove from heat and serve immediately.

9. Tuna Wrap
Serves 2

Ingredients

- 1 can albacore tuna
- 1 ripe avocado
- 1 small scallion finely chopped
- 2 large leaves of lettuce
- ½ cup raw mushrooms finely chopped

Directions

In a bowl mash the avocado until it's a creamy consistency. Add the tuna, the mushrooms and the scallions. Mix all together. In a large lettuce leaf place a scoop of the mixture and wrap. Repeat the process with the second leaf.

10.   Squash Pasta
Serves 4

Ingredients

- 4 yellow medium squash
- 1 tablespoon olive oil
- ¼ cup Pine nuts
- Salt and Pepper as desired.

Directions

Use a julienne peeler to slice the squash into noodles. Stop when you reach the seeds. Heat the olive oil in a skillet, place the squash noodles and sauté over medium heat for 3-4 minutes.
Add salt and pepper as desired. Top with pine nuts.

Dinner

1. Cauliflower Rice with Shrimp
Serves 2-3

Ingredients

- 1 large head of Cauliflower
- ½ onion finely chopped
- 1 garlic clove finely chopped
- 1 tablespoon coconut oil
- Salt and Pepper as desired
- 1 lb. Peeled and Washed Shrimp

Directions

Remove leaves and stem from cauliflower. Grate the remainder of the cauliflower head until it resembles rice.
Add coconut oil to skillet and set to medium heat. Introduce the shrimp, onion and garlic until slightly brown and shrimp is fully cooked. Add in grated cauliflower, salt and pepper and stir until heated. Serve immediately.

2. Baked Salmon with asparagus
Serves 4

Ingredients

- 4 wild salmon steaks
- 1 lemon sliced
- 1 garlic clove finely chopped
- ½ cup fresh dill
- 16 sprigs of asparagus
- Salt and Pepper as desired
- 2 tablespoons olive oil

Directions

Preheat the oven to 350 degrees Fahrenheit. In a baking sheet prepare 4 medium size aluminum foils, these should be big enough to place the salmon. Place the salmon in each foil, place salt and pepper as desired. Drizzle ½ tablespoon on each salmon, rub with garlic and dill. Place 1 slice of lemon in each foil. Close the foil and place in the oven for 30 minutes. Remove from the oven, allow to cool 5 minutes. In a separate foil place the asparagus for 5 minutes in the oven with salt, pepper and a light drizzle of olive oil. Serve both together immediately.

3. Mashed Cauliflower
Serves 3-4

Ingredients

- 1 head of cauliflower
- ¼ cup almond milk
- ½ garlic clove finely chopped
- Salt and pepper as desired
- 4 cups water
- ¼ cups parsley

Directions

Boil the water with salt in the pot. Add the cauliflower and boil until tender. Remove the water and mash the cauliflower. Add the almond milk and garlic and mix together. Allow to simmer for 3 minutes. Top with parsley. You may serve this with steak, chicken or fish.

4. Garlic Shrimp
Serves 4-6

Ingredients

- ½ cup olive oil
- 5 garlic cloves thinly sliced
- 1 lb. raw shrimp peeled and deveined
- ½ teaspoon paprika
- ¼ tablespoon red flakes pepper (if you like it spicy)

Directions

Heat the olive oil in skillet on low to medium heat. Add garlic and sauté for 3 minutes, stirring frequently. Add the shrimp, salt and paprika. Increase the temperature to medium-high.
Cook for 4 minutes on each side. Serve warm.

5. Zucchini Bolognese
Serves 2-3

Ingredients

- 1 lb. ground beef
- 3 medium zucchini
- ½ onion chopped finely
- 3 ripe tomatoes cubed
- 5 bay leaves
- ½ tablespoon olive oil
- Salt and Pepper as desired

Directions

Use a julienne peeler to slice the zucchini into noodles. Stop when you reach the seeds. In a skillet place the olive oil and heat to medium to high. Add the onions for 2 minutes and add the ground beef. Add salt and pepper as desired. Ina separate sauce pan place the 3 tomatoes with the bay leaves to a high heat. Cook for 5 minutes. Once the ground beef is thoroughly cooked, 8-10 minutes add the tomato sauce and the zucchini. Mix all ingredients together and remove from heat. Serve immediately.

6. Chicken with Olives
Serves 3-4

Ingredients

- 3 skinless and boneless chicken breasts
- 2 tablespoons olives
- 1 cup chicken broth
- Salt as desired

Directions

Heat olive oil on skillet to medium heat. Place chicken and sauté until brown on both sides. Add the broth and olives. Allow to cook for another 7-8 minutes depending on the thickness of the chicken. Place the chicken on the serving plate. Leave the broth and olives on high heat until it thicken 3-4 minutes. Place the sauce on the chicken. Serve immediately.

7. Lettuce Turkey Burgers
Serves 4 burgers

Ingredients

- 1 lb. ground turkey
- ¼ cup onion finely chopped
- Salt and Pepper as desired
- 1 tablespoon coconut oil
- 4 Large Lettuce leaves

Directions
In a large bowl mix the turkey, salt, pepper and onions together with a fork. With this mixture form 4 patties. Heat skillet to medium-high heat and add the coconut oil. Cook the burgers until browned on both sides time depends on the term desired. Remove from skillet and allow to cool for 5 minutes. Wrap each burger with a large lettuce leaf.

8. Double Noodle Beef
Serves 2-3

Ingredients

- 1 onion diced
- 2 cups kale or spinach finely chopped
- 1 zucchini julienne sliced
- 1 squash julienne sliced
- 1 lb. flank steak stir fry sliced
- 1 tablespoon coconut oil
- Salt as desired.

Directions

Heat skillet to medium-high heat and add coconut oil. Add the steak and onion to the skillet. Cook until brown for around 5-6 minutes. Add the spinach or kale, squash and zucchini. Stir consistently for 2-3 minutes. Serve warm.

9. Caveman Steak

Serves 2

Ingredients

- 2 slices of strip steak 1" thick
- 1 Teaspoon Garlic minced
- Salt and pepper as desired
- 1 Tablespoon Coconut Oil
- ½ cup parsley finely chopped

Directions

Preheat broiler to high. In a separate bowl mix the salt, pepper, coconut oil, garlic and parsley. Place the steaks on a broiler pan and brush both sides of the steak with the mixture from the bowl. Broil 8 minutes for medium term, turn steaks and cook for another 5 minutes.

Remove from the oven and cover for 5 minutes. Serve with your vegetables of choice.

10. Rainbow Salad
Serves 3-4

Ingredients

- 2 cups Mixed greens (spinach, kale, lettuce)
- 1 cup broccoli
- 1 cup cauliflower
- ½ cup Purple cabbage
- ½ cup Red Bell Pepper
- ½ cup Red Apple slices
- 12 cherry tomatoes
- 1 tablespoon lemon juice
- 1 tablespoon olive oil
- ¼ cup walnuts

Directions

Chop the Cabbage and bell pepper into small sized pieces. Also cut the broccoli and cauliflower into bite sized florets. In a Salad bowl combine all the ingredients and toss with the lemon juice and olive oil. Top the salad with the apple slices and the walnuts.

Snacks

1. Sweet and Nutty Smoothie
Serves 1-2

Ingredients

- 1 cup almond milk
- ½ cup spinach
- ½ banana
- 1 cup strawberries
- 3 tablespoons almond butter

Directions
Place all ingredients into blender. Blend.
Enjoy!

2. Turkey Balls
Serves 4-6

Ingredients

- 1 lb. ground turkey
- ½ onion finely chopped
- 1 garlic clove finely chopped
- ½ cup parsley finely chopped
- ½ spinach or kale finely chopped
- Salt and Pepper as desired

Directions

Preheat oven to 350 degrees Fahrenheit. Put all the ingredients into a large mixing bowl and mix everything together. Using your hands form small balls with the mixture and place those onto a baking sheet.

Bake the turkey balls for around 20 minutes or until they are lightly browned. Allow to cool down for 5 minutes and serve.

3. Fruit Roll ups
Serves 10 strips

Ingredients

- 2 apples finely chopped
- 10 strawberries finely chopped
- 1 orange cubed
- 1 teaspoon cinnamon
- ¼ cup water
- 1 tablespoon honey

Directions

Add the water to a pot and bring to a boil. Add the fruit and reduce the heat to a simmer. Cook until the fruit is soft and the water has been reduced. Mix in the cinnamon and honey. Transfer the fruit to a blender and puree until smooth. If you need more sweetness, you may add more honey.

Preheat oven to 250 degrees Fahrenheit. Smooth the fruit mixture over a baking tray lined with baking paper. Spread evenly to cover the entire surface. Bake for 8 hours. Lt it cool completely before peeling off the fruit from the tray. You can store it in an airtight container for up to 1 week.

4. Kale Chips
Serves 2-3

Ingredients

- 4 cups of chopped kale washed and dried
- 2 tablespoons olive oil
- Salt as desired

Directions

Preheat oven to 300 degrees Fahrenheit. Toss the kale with the olive oil and salt. Spread on a baking sheet and bake for 12-15 minutes. Remove from the oven and allow to cool slightly before serving.

4. Baked Sweet Potato Chips
Serves 2-3

Ingredients

- 2 large sweet potatoes peeled and thinly sliced
- 2 tablespoons coconut oil
- 1 teaspoon rosemary
- Salt as desired

Directions

Preheat oven to 375 degrees Fahrenheit. Toss sweet potatoes with coconut oil, rosemary and salt. Spread on a baking sheet and bake for 10 minutes then flip over chips and bake for 10 more minutes.

5. Energy Bar
Serves 2-3

Ingredients

- 1 cup almonds
- 1 cup dried cranberries
- 1 cup pitted dates
- 1 tablespoon unsweetened coconut flakes
- ¼ cup small dark chocolate chips

Directions

Combine all of the ingredients in a blender or food processor. Blend until all ingredients are broken down and begin to clump together. Place the mixture on a piece of baking paper or plastic wrap. Press into an even square and chill wrapped for 1 hour. Enjoy!

6. Figs with Prosciutto
Serves 3-4

Ingredients

- 6 black figs
- 12 basil leaves
- 12 slices prosciutto
- 1 tablespoon olive oil
- 1 toothpicks

Directions

Preheat the oven to 375 degrees Fahrenheit. In a baking sheet line it with baking paper and brush with olive oil. Cut the figs in half. Place a basil leaf on the inside of each fig, then wrap with a slice of prosciutto. Secure both with a toothpick.

Bake for 10 minutes, rotating the pan at 5 minutes time. Serve warm.

7. Shrimp Ceviche
Serves 4

Ingredients

- 1 lb. uncooked shrimp peeled and deveined
- 3 tablespoon olive oil
- ½ cup Lemon juice
- 1 cup orange juice
- 1 red onion finely sliced
- 3 tomatoes cubed
- ½ cup cilantro
- Salt and Pepper as desired
- 1 organic tomato paste
- 1 cup water

Directions

Place water to boil in a pan, once it's boiling add shrimp and cook for 5 minutes. Remove from heat and cool. In a separate bowl combine olive oil, lemon juice, orange juice, red onion, tomatoes, tomato paste and water. Mix well until all ingredients are well combined. Add the shrimp. For best results refrigerate overnight before serving.

8. Simple Prosciutto Melon Slices
Serves 2

Ingredients

- 1/4 ripe melon peeled and sliced
- 50 grams prosciutto
- Balsamic vinegar if desired

Directions

Cut each prosciutto slice until they measure 1" to 2" in width and maintain the length. Wrap each slice of melon with a slice of prosciutto. If desired you may dip into balsamic vinegar for extra flavor.

9. Baked Eggs in Portobello Mushrooms
Serves 2

Ingredients

- 2 eggs
- 2 large Portobello caps
- ½ teaspoon olive oil
- 1 slice pancetta or prosciutto

Directions

Preheat oven to 375 degrees Fahrenheit. Clean the mushroom and scrape out stems and gills so it's deep enough for the egg. Rub the mushrooms with olive oil. On the inside of the eggs place ½ slice of prosciutto or pancetta. Place the eggs on the baking dish. Carefully open the egg and place inside the mushroom cap. Place in the oven for 20-30 minutes, depending on how you like your eggs. Serve immediately.

10. Banana Sushi

Serves 1-2

Ingredients

- 1 large ripe banana
- 3 tablespoons almond butter
- ½ tablespoon chopped almonds
- ½ tablespoon Chia Seeds

Directions

Peel your banana and spread the almond butter covering only 1 side of the banana. On the side covered with almond butter sprinkle chia seeds and chopped almonds, gently press them into the butter. Cut the banana in round several slices and place in the freezer for 1 hour before serving.

Dessert

1. Raw Brownie Treats

Serves 4-5

Ingredients

- 2 cups walnuts
- 1 cup pitted dates
- 1 teaspoon vanilla
- 1/3 cup unsweetened cocoa powder

Directions

Blend the walnuts in a blender or food processor until the walnuts are finely ground. Add the dates, vanilla and cocoa powder. Mix well until everything is combined. Add several drops of water to get the mixture to stick together. Transfer the mix to a separate bowl. Using your hands make small cubes. Enjoy! You may store them in the refrigerator for up to a week.

2. Chocolate Cake in a Mug
Serves 1

Ingredients

- 1 tablespoon almond flour
- 1 tablespoon unsweetened cocoa powder
- 1 tablespoon almond milk
- 1 tablespoon honey
- 1 teaspoon vanilla
- 1 egg

Directions

Combine all ingredients in a mug, mix well and microwave for 1 to 1.5 minutes. Serve with fresh berries if desired.

3. Grilled Nectarines with Coconut Cream
Serves 4

Ingredients

- 2 medium nectarines cut in half and pitted
- 1 teaspoon vanilla
- ¼ cup chopped walnuts
- 1 can coconut milk
- Cinnamon as desired

Directions

On a skillet grill nectarines on medium to high heat around 3-5 minute son each side starting with the cut side down. Use the cream from the top of the coconut milk can and whisk together with vanilla. Drizzle the cream over each nectarine. Top with cinnamon and walnuts as desired.

4. Strawberry Banana Ice cream
Serves 3-4

Ingredients

- 3 ripe bananas peeled, sliced and frozen
- 2 tablespoon honey
- ½ cup almond milk
- 3 tablespoon almond butter
- ½ cup strawberries frozen

Directions

Place all ingredients in the blender and gently blend until it reaches the desired consistency. You may serve with dark chocolate or sliced almonds.

5. Chocolate Chip Cookies
Serves 3-4

Ingredients

- 1 cup macadamias
- 1 cup dates pitted
- 1 tablespoon cacao

Directions

Preheat oven to 350 degrees Fahrenheit.
Line a baking tray with baking paper.

In a blender combine all ingredients and
mix until they begin to stick together. Using
your hands roll the mixture into small balls,
place on the baking tray and slightly flatten.
Bake for 10 minutes. Allow to cool
completely before serving.

6. Chocolate Pudding
Serves 2

Ingredients

- 1 ripe avocado
- 3 tablespoons cocoa powder
- 4 tablespoons honey
- 1 teaspoon vanilla
- 3 tablespoons almond milk

Directions

Place all the ingredients into a blender or food processor and blend until smooth and creamy. Place in a serving plate in the refrigerator for 30 minutes before eating.

7. Almond Butter Sweets
Serves 12

Ingredients

- 1 cup almond butter
- 1 tablespoon honey
- 1 tablespoon coconut oil
- 1 cup 70% dark chocolate

Directions
Place almond butter, oil and honey in a pot at low heat until melted. Place a spoonful into a mini muffin baking pan. Place the dark chocolate in pan at low heat until melted. Drizzle the dark chocolate on top of the almond butter. Place in the freezer for 30 minutes, remove from freezer and enjoy.

8. Coconut Macaroon
Serves 4

Ingredients

- ½ cup coconut oil
- ½ cup coconut butter
- 1 cup shredded coconut
- 3 tablespoons honey

Directions
Heat the coconut oil and butter in a very low heat, until they are soft. Remove from heat. Add the honey and mix well. Add the shredded coconut gradually until you get the consistency you want. Shape the macaroons into small balls or any desired shape and allow them to cool down. Enjoy!

9. Easy Chocolate Truffles
Serves 8 Truffles

Ingredients

- 4 dates, pitted and halved
- ½ teaspoon coconut oil
- 8 pecan halves
- 1/3 cup 70% dark chocolate

Directions
Melt the chocolate in a pot with the coconut oil in a very light heat. Press a pecan half into each of the date halves. Then dip the date with the pecan inside the dark chocolate. Allow to cool for 15 minutes in the freezer before serving.

10. Cocoa Mousse
Serves 4

Ingredients

- 5 tablespoons cocoa powder
- 3 tablespoons honey
- 1 teaspoon vanilla extract
- 2 chilled cans coconut milk

Directions

Scrape the cream off the top of both the cans of coconut milk. Place it in a bowl and add cocoa, vanilla and honey. Begin to mix with electric mixer at medium-high speed until peaks begin to form, around 5 minutes. Divide the mixture into serving bowls and refrigerate until ready to serve.

9 781533 670335